THE RED VIOLIN CAPRICES

edited by *Joshua Bell*

Variation 2
(A) **Con bravura**

ad lib.

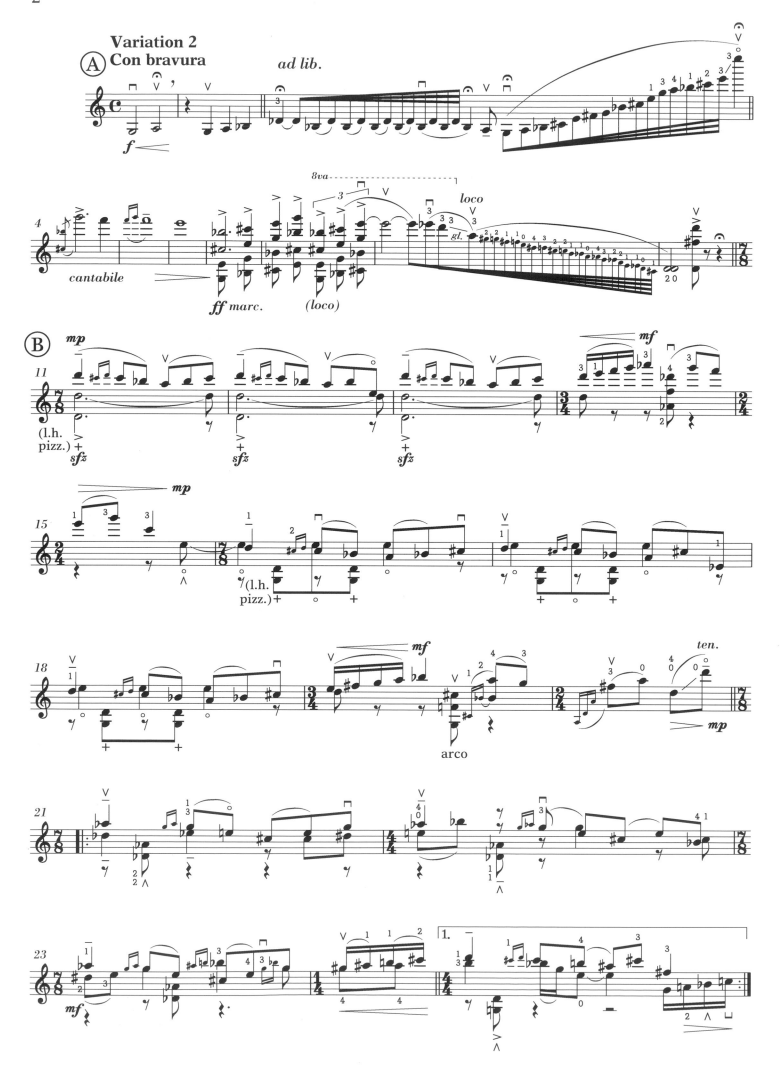

JOHN CORIGLIANO

THE RED VIOLIN CAPRICES

for solo violin

ED 4095
first printing: July 2001

ISBN 978-0-634-00184-0

G. SCHIRMER, Inc.

DISTRIBUTED BY

HAL•LEONARD®
CORPORATION
7777 W. BLUEMOUND RD. P.O. BOX 13819 MILWAUKEE, WI 53213

PROGRAM NOTE

These Caprices, composed in conjunction with the score for François Girard's film *The Red Violin*, take a spacious, troubadour-inspired theme and vary it both linearly and stylistically. These variations intentionally evoke Baroque, Gypsy, and arch-Romantic idioms as they examine the same materials (a dark, seven-chord chaconne as well as that principal theme) from differing aural viewpoints. The Caprices were created and ordered to reflect the structure of the film, in which Bussotti, a fictional 18th-century violin maker, crafts his greatest violin for his soon-to-be-born son. When tragedy claims wife and child, the grief-stricken Bussotti, in a gesture both ardent and macabre, infuses the blood of his beloved into the varnish of the instrument. Their fates thus joined, the violin travels across three centuries through Vienna, London, Shanghai and Montreal, passing through the hands of a doomed child prodigy, a flamboyant virtuoso, a haunted Maoist commissar, and at last a willful Canadian expert, whose own plans for the violin finally complete the circle of parent and child united in art.

– JOHN CORIGLIANO

The Red Violin Caprices *are derived from*
John Corigliano's music for The Red Violin, *which received*
the 1999 Academy Award for Best Original Score.

The Caprices *were composed especially for Joshua Bell.*
The film soundtrack (Sony Classical 63010) features Joshua Bell
with Esa-Pekka Salonen conducting the Philharmonia Orchestra.

duration: ca. 10 minutes

related works available from the publisher
The Red Violin: Suite *(solo violin, strings, harp & percussion)*
The Red Violin: Chaconne *(solo violin & orchestra)*
the Chaconne *is also available in a reduction for violin & piano*

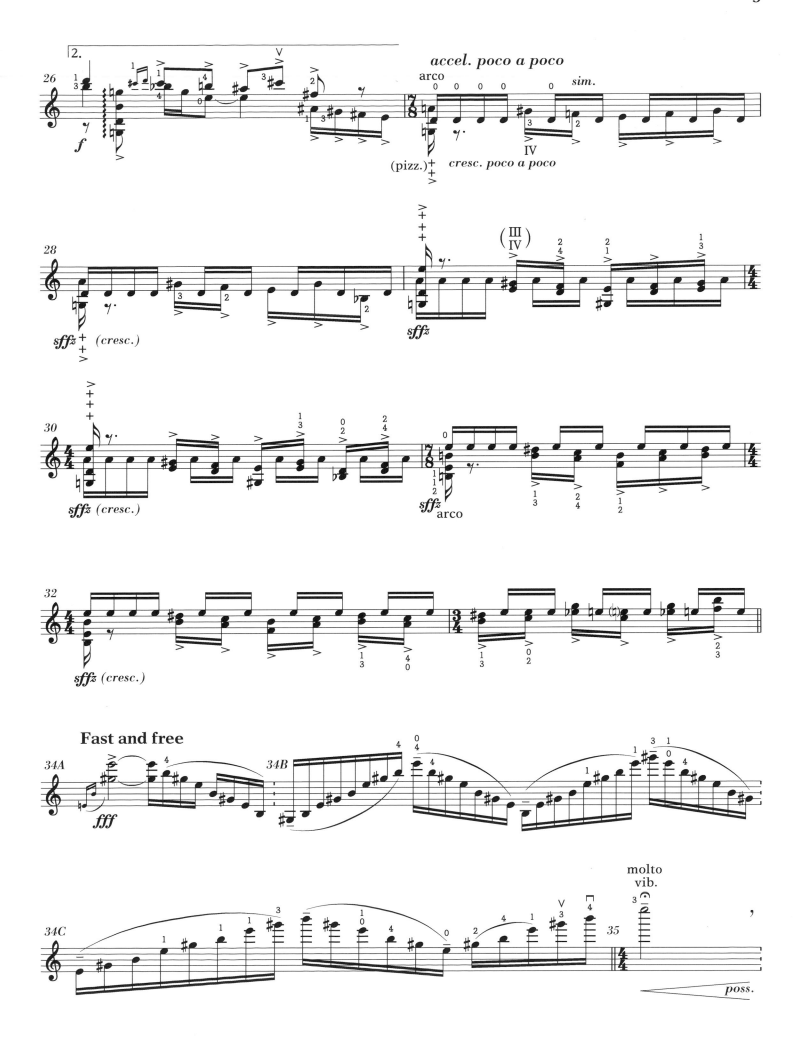

Variation 3
Adagio, languid

Variation 4
Slowly con rubato

♩ = ca. 60–66

Faster ♩ = ca. 80

Tempo I (♩ = ca. 60–66)

Faster ♩ = 80

attacca

6

Variation 5
Presto, pesante

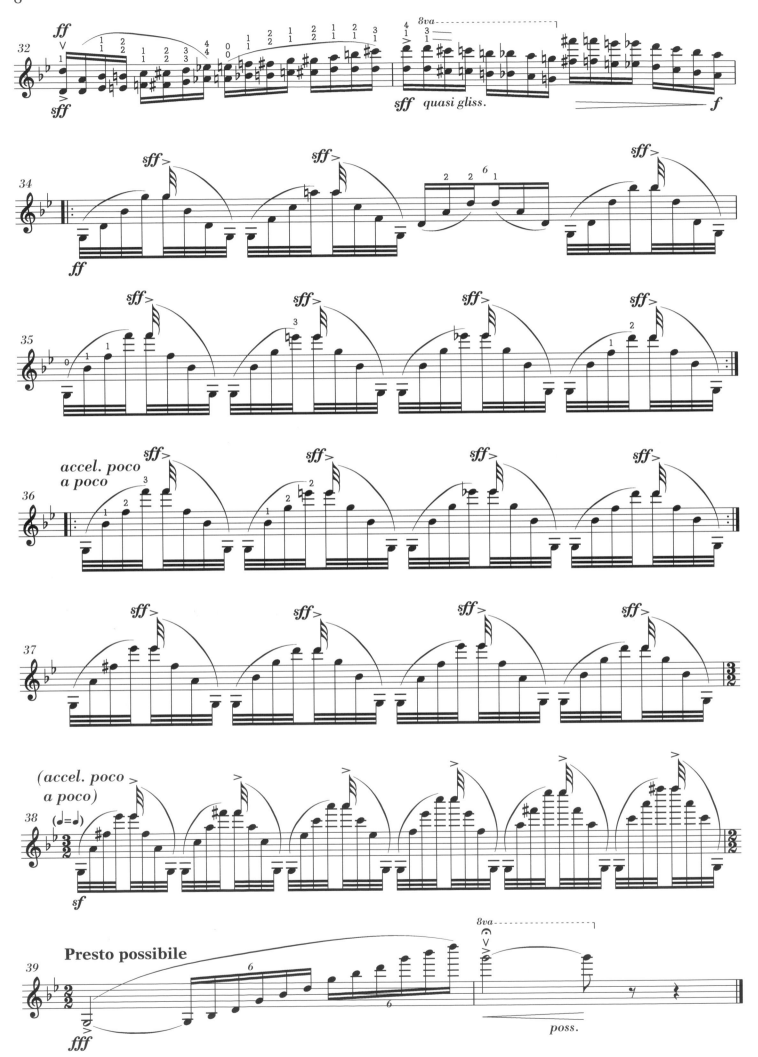

JOHN CORIGLIANO

THE RED VIOLIN CAPRICES

for solo violin

G. SCHIRMER, Inc.

DISTRIBUTED BY